Therefore submit to God. Resist the devil and he will flee from you.

James 4:7

YOUR WORD IS A LAMP TO MY FEET AND A LIGHT FOR MY PATH.

PSALM 119:105

IN ALL YOUR WAYS ACKNOWLEDGE HIM, AND HE WILL MAKE YOUR PATHS STRAIGHT. PROVERBS 3:6

IN EVERYTHING HE DID HE HAD GREAT SUCCESS, BECAUSE THE LORD WAS WITH HIM.

1 SAMUEL 18:14

Delight yourself also in the Lord, and he shall give you the desires of your heart.
Psalm 37:4

FOR THE SPIRIT GOD GAVE US DOES NOT MAKE US TIMID, BUT GIVES US POWER, LOVE AND SELF-DISCIPLINE.

2 TIMOTHY 1:7

BUT THE FRUIT OF THE SPIRIT IS LOVE, JOY, PEACE, KINDNESS, GOODNESS, FAITHFULNESS

GALATIANS 5:22

I AM THE WAY THE TRUTH AND THE LIFE. NO ONE COMES TO THE FATHER EXCEPT THROUGH ME.

JOHN 14:6

Made in the USA
Monee, IL
23 July 2025

21766660R00046